# SOUTH TEXAS
# WILDFLOWERS

## COLLECTION ONE

TEXT BY HAL HAM
ILLUSTRATED BY MARTHA BRUCE

Published by the Conner Museum
Texas A&I University
Kingsville, Texas

This publication is made possible as part of a grant from the
Caesar Kleberg Foundation for Wildlife Conservation.

Editor:  Joan Pendleton

Designer:  Dee Azadian

Cover Photo:  Water Hyacinth
by Lloyd Logan

International Standard Book Number 0-916983-00-5

10/M Office of Public Affairs, Publications & Information Services

Printed in the United States of America
Golden Banner Press, Inc.

# PREFACE

South Texas is noted for the variety, abundance, and beauty of its spring wildflowers. I hope this book will convey some of that beauty and diversity. Fortunately, Mrs. Jimmie Picquet, the director of the John E. Conner Museum, perceived a value to this effort and provided unstinting support and encouragement for the project. I am deeply indebted.

Ms. Martha Bruce's artistry in rendering slides and dried specimens into vibrant representations of technical and esthetic beauty is the cornerstone of this book. I am constantly impressed by her talent and technique.

Most of the flowers portrayed in the succeeding pages of this book were painted from slides taken by Mr. Lloyd Logan. He devoted considerable time, effort, and expertise to this book, and I am very grateful for his assistance.

Dr. George Williges of the Department of Biology, Texas A&I University, provided access to the herbarium and to his own great knowledge of South Texas flora during the compilation of this book. This was not a small factor, and his assistance and advice are gratefully noted.

I am also indebted to Dr. Marshall C. Johnston of the Department of Botany at the University of Texas for his invaluable assistance with current nomenclature and his review of the plates and identifications.

Dr. Edwin Bogusch, with the assistance of his wife Ethel, has contributed a section to this book. They have spent many years studying and learning the wildflowers of South Texas, and I am pleased to include their portion in this book.

Finally, Joan Pendleton and Dee Azadian who, respectively, edited and designed this book, have my deepest appreciation for their time, effort, and professionalism.

March 1, 1984
Hal Ham

# CONTENTS

# INTRODUCTION

This book is intended to be a casual guide for identifying some of the wildflowers of South Texas. To that end we include 29 plates depicting 85 flowers arranged by color, starting with red and moving through the spectrum to white.

To use this guide, go to the color plates and find the picture that most closely matches the specimen you have. One drawback to this method is the variety of colors that many species of flowers display. If you can't identify your flower by matching colors, try to find a flower that is similar to your specimen and read the description on the facing page that will tell you more about that flower, including color phases. There will also be information on the habitat and other characteristics of the flower, most particularly measurements of various kinds. As these measurements are in millimeters (mm), centimeters (cm), and meters (m), a metric rule of 22 cm may be found on page 71.

The 85 flowers pictured, with some species repeated, are only a few of the hundreds that bloom in South Texas in the spring. While many flowers in this book are commonly found, many more are not. If you wish to go more deeply into the identification of wildflowers, several other resources are available. The following publications will all help identify wildflowers and were also used extensively in the compilation of this book.

*Roadside Flowers of Texas,* paintings by Mary Motz Wills and text by Howard S. Irwin. Published by the University of Texas Press at Austin, this book covers the whole state and has 257 flowers reproduced in color as well as a taxonomic key. A good book for more extensive coverage of the state, it is easily found at bookstores and in libraries.

*Flora of the Texas Coastal Bend,* by Fred B. Jones. This is a floral key published by the Rob and Bessie Welder Wildlife Foundation in 1977. All of the flowers in our book may be found in this key. For those inspired to consult a key, as is occasionally recommended, this is likely to be the best choice. There are some line drawings by Eveline Jackson.

*Wild Flowers of the United States* Volume 3, Parts 1 & 2, "Texas," by Harold William Rickett. This publication of the New York Botanical Garden has color photographs of most of the wildflowers in Texas and is also keyed to help begin the search. It is a highly recommended guide and can probably be found in libraries.

*Wild Flowers of the United States* Volume 2, Parts 1 & 2, "The Southeastern States," by Harold William Rickett. Volume 2 of the series mentioned above, this covers some plants not included in volume 3.

*Manual of the Vascular Plants of Texas,* by Donovan Stewart Correll and Marshall Conring Johnston. This publication by the University of Texas at Dallas is a highly technical floral key that covers all the plants in Texas. It is the final authority, but difficult for casual taxonomists to use.

An additional guide to plants of South Texas that covers some grasses and shrubs as well as what we are considering wildflowers is *Common Wetland Plants of Southeast Texas,* a publication of the U.S. Army Corps of Engineers, Galveston District. It is intended to be a nontechnical guide to wetland plants and includes color photographs.

# PHLOX

*Phlox drummondii*

**Phlox Family: Polemoniaceae**

This annual is widespread and locally abundant. Several species and sub-species all have similarly shaped flowers. The corolla of *P. drummondii* is 1.5-2.5 cm wide with leaves 1-7 cm long, and the entire plant ranges from 10 to 50 cm high; it has erect to trailing stems and generally grows in masses. Because this is a popular cultivated variety of flower and some of the cultivated types may be found growing wild, a wide range of colors may be found. Purple, lavender, rose, and pink of various shades are common, but hybridization and habitat factors make colors widely variable within and between the species. The other common species in this area is *P. glabriflora.* The phloxes prefer sandier soils and will bloom from February to June and occasionally into fall.

PHLOX

# CORAL BEAN

*Erythrina herbacea*

**Pea Family: Fabaceae (Leguminosae)**

A perennial woody-based shrub or sub-shrub, this prickly or thorny plant grows 2 m or more high. This plant will flower from erect leafless shoots, March to May. The upper petal is 3-5 cm long. It is frequent in sandy soils closer to the coast and is also commonly cultivated. The leaves produced later in the spring are three-foliate (three leaflets per leaf). The seeds produced are also red and are poisonous. The Spanish name is Colorin.

# SCARLET SAGE

*Salvia coccinea*

**Mint Family: Lamiaceae (Labiatae)**

This commonly occurring herbaceous perennial grows up to 1 m high, the stems erect. The corolla is 2-2.5 cm long and may rarely be pink or white. The preferred habitat is sandy or loamy soils or caliche, and it is frequently shaded. The flowering period in South Texas can be from March to December. This sage is known by other common names: Indian-fire and Tropical Sage or, in Spanish, Mirto or Mejorana.

# INDIAN PAINTBRUSH

*Castilleja indivisa*

**Figwort Family: Scrophulariaceae**

This very attractive annual or weak perennial wildflower is frequently seen in large masses in full sun along roadsides and in fields of sandy soils. Of the species found in the state, *indivisa* is the one most likely to be encountered in South Texas. The petals of this species are inconspicuous, the colorful red being modified leaves, called bracts, which surround the petals. These plants are erect and from 10 to 14 cm high with leaves from 3 to 10 cm long. In some areas pink and white colorations can be found. Also called Texas or Scarlet Paintbrush, it blooms from March to May or June and sometimes in the fall.

CORAL BEAN

SCARLET SAGE

INDIAN PAINTBRUSH

# WINECUP

*Callirhoë involucrata*

**Mallow Family: Malvaceae**

One of two species generally found in South Texas, *C. involucrata* has stems that are decumbent, trailing along the ground. They may be 1 m or more in length, and the flowers occur in a solitary fashion along the stem. The corolla, all of the petals, is 4-6 cm in diameter and white on the inside toward the base. This perennial blooms from February to June on deep sands or gravelly soils in prairies and along roads; it can be locally very abundant. *C. leiocarpa* produces a very similar flower but on a large, 1-m high bush.

# INDIAN BLANKET

*Gaillardia pulchella*

**Sunflower Family: Asteraceae (Compositae)**

This is an annual herb up to 60 cm tall usually with branches from near the base. The flowering heads are from 3.5 to 5.5 cm wide and display a wide variety of petal coloration. The ray flowers, those surrounding the central disk, vary from solid red to red-tipped with yellow to solid yellow. It is one of the most common and characteristic of the spring flowers and can cover fields and roadsides. Most frequent in the spring and early summer on sandy soils and prairies, it prefers sunshine. It is also called Firewheel.

# CARDINAL FEATHER

*Acalypha radians*

**Spurge Family: Euphorbiaceae**

A low-growing perennial (to 30 cm high) with many branches forming clumps or mound shapes, this plant has the male and female flowers on different plants. Drawn is the female, showing the feathery red styles. It can be locally abundant on dry sandy or gravelly sites or island dunes. The male plant is not so attractive, having compact reddish spikes to 3 cm long. This plant begins flowering in March and some may still be found into late fall.

WINECUP                                    INDIAN BLANKET

CARDINAL FEATHER

# WILD HONEYSUCKLE

*Gaura sp.*

**Evening-Primrose Family: Onagraceae**

Several species of *Gaura* are found in this area. Occurring on various soils, these generally erect plants, from 60 cm to 1.2 m high, are easily recognized by the arrangement of their flowers into spikes or panicles, such as depicted, and the general aging of the flowers from white to pink or red. Some species are frequent in occurrence. Most begin blooming in March and continue until July or later.

# WILD ONION

*Allium drummondii*

**Lily Family: Liliaceae**

One of several species of wild onion in the area, *A. drummondii* is usually from 10 to 35 cm high and will have from 10 to 25 flowers, which can be white, pink, lavender, or reddish purple. It can be common on heavier sands, clay, or caliche. It is easily identified as an onion by the smell. This species is also called Prairie Onion or Cebollita.

# PRICKLY POPPY

*Argemone sanguinea*

**Poppy Family: Papaveraceae**

A prickly, stinging, erect herbaceous annual to 1 m or more high, this species has two color phases (white and purple or lavender), and petals 3-4 cm long. In some areas it is an abundant although an attractive pest. It occurs in disturbed areas and fields on various soils and frequently along roadsides. May also be called Red Poppy.

WILD HONEYSUCKLE                          WILD ONION

PRICKLY POPPY

# BULL THISTLE

*Cirsium horridulum*

**Sunflower Family: Asteraceae (Compositae)**

Great variability in height is common with this annual or weak biennial thistle; it may flower at heights of 20 cm to more than 1 m. The spiny leaves are 15-30 cm long. The flowering head is generally solitary but there may be two or three heads. The flower is most commonly pink but may be lavender, purple, or white and is 4.5-6 cm tall. It is distinguished from Texas Thistle, below, by the spiny bracts that enclose the flowering head. It is frequently encountered on deep sands and in open places from March to June.

# TEXAS THISTLE

*Cirsium texanum*

**Sunflower Family: Asteraceae (Compositae)**

Texas Thistle is similar to Bull Thistle; the most observable difference is the absence of spiny bracts surrounding the head. Texas Thistle is also an annual or weak biennial with the flowering heads solitary on the stem. The heads are 3-4 cm high. It can become extremely abundant in localized areas, generally disturbed areas, and roadsides from February to June. Both Texas Thistle and Bull Thistle can be easily identified by the severe stinging sensation they produce when touched.

# SENSITIVE BRIAR

*Schrankia latidens*

**Pea Family: Fabaceae (Leguminosae)**

Of the several similiar-looking species of sensitive briar that may be encountered, *S. latidens* is the most probable discovery. The stems that trail along the ground or clamber upward on other vegetation are 1 m or more long and have small thorns or prickles. The globular heads, 1.5-2 cm wide, are generally the color depicted but may be more lavender or rose. Each leaf is divided into 2 to 5 or 6 parts, pinnae, with each of those parts having 6 to 13 pairs of leaflets. The plant takes its name from the folding-together action of each pair of leaflets when touched or otherwise disturbed. This perennial, which grows from a woody rootstock, prefers sandy soils in prairies and openings and on island dunes where it can be found frequently. It flowers from April to September or October. *S. roemeriana* and *S. uncinata* are two other sensitive briars you might encounter.

BULL THISTLE                    TEXAS THISTLE

SENSITIVE BRIAR

# EVENING-PRIMROSE

*Oenothera speciosa*

**Evening-Primrose Family: Onagraceae**

Many species and even another genus, *Calylophus,* go by the general name of Evening-primrose. Many of these are yellow-flowered and the others are white or pink. *O. speciosa* as depicted is abundant and widespread in South Texas, forming extensive colonies by rhizomes. The stems are erect to reclining and 30 cm or more long. The petals are 2.5-4 cm long and may also be white or rose. This flower is also known as Pink Evening-primrose, Primrose, Showy Primrose, and Amapola del Campo. Because so many Evening-primroses abound, a floral key should be consulted for a definite identification of a flower that doesn't look like the one pictured. The Evening-primroses may be quickly separated into genera by examining the stigma. The stigma of *Calylophus* is disk-shaped and that of *Oenothera* split into five individual parts.

# JUSTICIA

*Justicia pilosella (Siphonoglossa pilosella)*

**Acanthus Family: Acanthaceae**

This small, low, woody-based perennial grows no higher than 30 cm and is often shorter. The leaves are 1-4 cm long. The stems are upright to prostrate and the corolla is about 2.5 cm long. The plant may be found in various soils and is frequently shaded. It may occasionally be found in abundance but is somewhat inconspicuous. The corolla is easily detached from the plant. *J. greggii* closely resembles *J. pilosella* but is more infrequently encountered. Both species flower from February to December.

# SKELETON PLANT

*Lygodesmia texana*

**Sunflower Family: Asteraceae (Compositae)**

An easily recognized perennial as high as 60 cm, this is the only species of this genus in South Texas. The leaves form a basal rosette and are narrow and toothed. The flowering head is solitary and 3-4.5 cm wide. It is a fairly frequent find on sandy loams or caliche soils and blooms from April to December.

SKELETON PLANT

# TEXAS VERVAIN

*Verbena halei*

**Verbena Family: Verbenaceae**

South Texas has many vervains. The vervains have now been separated into two genera, and representatives of both groups are pictured. *V. halei* and other *Verbena* have flowers arranged in spikes. The corolla of Texas Vervain is 5-8 mm wide and colored from lavender to light blue or purplish. This is a perennial species that grows up to 1 m high on various soils from February to November or December. It is frequently abundant and easily seen on the roadside.

# MEXICAN VERVAIN

*Glandularia bipinnatifida (Verbena ciliata)*

**Verbena Family: Verbenaceae**

Mexican Vervain is an example of the vervains that have flowers arranged in clusters. This species often forms mats no more than 20 cm high from prostrate or reclining stems, several from a common base. The corolla is 6-13 mm wide and may be lavender, light blue-violet, or violet-purple. It is attractive and abundant along roads and in heavier sands and clay. It is mostly a spring bloomer, February to May, but may also bloom October through December. Other common names are Alfombrilla del Campo and Moradilla.

# MISTFLOWER

*Eupatorium bentonicifolium*

**Sunflower Family: Asteraceae (Compositae)**

A species of the genus called mistflower, *E. bentonicifolium* is a perennial with stems that are usually reclining, the lower nodes rooted. The stems are up to 1 m long with leaves of 2-4 cm in length. The heads are 6-9 mm high and may be of a slightly more blue-white hue. It is frequent in damp sand on the barrier islands and along the mainland coast where it blooms from April to December. Several species of the mistflower genus are found in South Texas and it is frequently difficult to tell certain of them apart.

TEXAS VERVAIN

MEXICAN VERVAIN

MISTFLOWER

# PALAFOXIA

*Palafoxia texana*

**Sunflower Family: Asteraceae (Compositae)**

One of two species of Palafoxia that might be encountered in South Texas, *P. texana* is an annual from 30 cm to 1.2 m high, with leaves 2-8 cm long and loosely clustered heads 10-15 cm high. These may be colored lavender, light purple, or purple-violet. It is fairly frequent and may be abundant in some areas, chiefly on sandy loamy soils and on beach shell. Beginning to bloom in April, it may continue through December with good conditions.


# SKULLCAP

*Scutellaria drummondii*

**Mint Family: Lamiaceae (Labiatae)**

Of the many Texas species of this genus, only a few occur in South Texas. *S. drummondii* grows to 30 cm high and, depending on the age and development of the plant, may have several to many branches from the base. The leaves are 5-20 mm long. The flowers are solitary, growing from the joint where the leaf meets the stem. The corolla is 6-13 mm long and may also be blue-violet. This species is widespread and frequent on various soils and habitats, blooming from February through November. Another species similar to Skullcap is Rattlesnake Flower, *Brazoria scutellarioides*. It can be distinguished from Skullcap by the lack of a protuberance on the upper side of the calyx.


# MEADOW-PINK

*Sabatia campestris*

**Gentian Family: Gentianaceae**

This annual has erect stems to 25 cm or slightly higher, generally unbranched on the lower half, with leaves 1.5-3.5 cm long. One of the more attractive wildflowers, it will occasionally be pale pink or white. This flower grows on damp sandy soils in openings and along roads and is a common find when it blooms from March through June or July. Another species, Salt-Marsh Pink *(S. arenicola)* is similar in appearance but is found closer to the coast and on the barrier islands. Where the two species intermix, hybrids may occur. The Meadow-Pink is also called the Texas Star.

PALAFOXIA                                    SKULLCAP

MEADOW-PINK

# ANEMONE

*Anemone heterophylla*

**Buttercup Family: Ranunculaceae**

Two species of Anemone occur in this area; the most common is *A. heterophylla*. One of the first wildflowers to bloom, it begins as early as January and continues until April. Botanically speaking, this plant has no petals; the delicate colors of white, pink, lavender, or purple are tepals. These petal-like appendages, which surround the reproductive portion of the flowering head, are borne on a stalk 10-40 cm high, a single "flower" on each. It can frequently be found in openings and prairies as well as along roads where the soil is clay or sandy clay.

# FALSE DRAGONHEAD

*Physostegia intermedia*

**Mint Family: Lamiaceae (Labiatae)**

Of several species of this genera found in Texas, only this one is likely to be found in South Texas. It is an annual about 1 m high, the leaves being 3-15 cm long. It is likely to be found in swales, ditches, and depressions and is occasionally abundant in an area toward the coast north of Rockport and east of Refugio. The genus as a whole is called Obedient-Plant.

# WILD PETUNIA

*Ruellia nudiflora*

**Acanthus Family: Acanthaceae**

Of the large number of Texas species in this genus, several are found in South Texas. *R. nudiflora* is a perennial growing 60 cm high, with leaves 3-20 cm long. An erect plant, the stems of older plants are woody toward the base. The flowers, which may be various shades of lavender or blue-violet, are 4.5-5.5 cm long. It is a frequent find in heavier soils. It blooms from April through November. A similar species, *R. yucatana*, has slightly smaller flowers and is frequently found around towns.

ANEMONE                          FALSE DRAGONHEAD

WILD PETUNIA

# LOOSESTRIFE

*Lythrum californicum*

**Loosestrife Family: Lythraceae**

This perennial grows about 60 cm high with leaves 1-6 cm long and petals 6-7 cm long. It will be found around water, along ditches, in moist sands in depressions, and swales. It is fairly common, blooming from March to July and occasionally on to fall. In Spanish it is known as Hierba del Cancer. *L. lanceolatum* may be encountered; its petals are shorter, 4-5 cm long, and colored lavender or light purple.


# HOARY PEA

*Tephrosia lindheimeri*

**Pea Family: Fabaceae (Leguminosae)**

This plant occurs occasionally on well-drained sands in prairies and open places. It is a perennial, growing from a woody base with weakly ascending stems 50 cm or more long and generally having 7-15 silvery gray leaflets per leaf. The upper blade of the petal is about 1.6 cm long. This *Tephrosia* is also called Goat's-rue and the roots and juice thereof are recorded as poisonous. Another species, *T. onobrychoides,* can be found frequently in coastal sands. The upper petal in this species is about 1.8 cm long, the corolla starting out white and aging to pink or purple.


# STORK'S BILL

*Erodium texanum*

**Geranium Family: Geraniaceae**

This annual herb has upright or ascending stems branched from the base to about 45 cm high. It occurs frequently on sands or caliche and along roads away from the coastal areas. There will generally be two or three flowers per flowering stem (peduncle), the petals 10-15 cm long. As a rule, the flowers open in the afternoon. The blooming period is from March to May. The reason for the common name will be apparent from the plate.

STORK'S BILL

# SNAKE HERB

*Dyschoriste linearis*

**Acanthus Family: Acanthaceae**

This fairly low perennial, to 30 cm high, has a few to several erect to ascending stems, leaves 1.5-5 cm long. The flowers, usually with two rows of purplish spots in the throat, are 1.5-2 cm long. It grows on various soils along roads and in openings or along bluffs and ravines. The flowering period is chiefly from April to July and occasionally into fall.

# BLUE CURLS

*Phacelia patuliflora*

**Waterleaf Family: Hydrophyllaceae**

This very attractive annual may form a carpetlike covering along the ground, generally not exceeding 30 cm in height. The flowers are borne in uncurling racemes, the corolla being 12-25 mm wide usually with the white center; the petals are lavender to purplish-violet or blue-violet. The leaves are oblong to broadly oval, 2-10 cm long. Of the several species in this genus, only three are likely to be found in South Texas. *P. laxa* is similar to *patuliflora* with a smaller corolla, 8-13 mm wide, and of pale violet-blue petals, noticeably paler than *patuliflora*.

# SPIDERWORT

*Tradescantia hirsutiflora*

**Spiderwort Family: Commelinaceae**

This genus comprises a number of species you might encounter, all perennials; some species require a floral key for identification. Interspecific hybrids are possible. *Hirsutiflora* will be 12-49 cm tall and have leaves 20 cm long or more. The petals are 1.2-1.5 cm long and may be blue-violet, purple, or rose. Not uncommon on loamy soils, it is often shaded while blooming from February to May.

SPIDERWORT

# CELESTIAL

*Trifurcia lahue (Alophia drummondii)*

**Iris Family: Iridaceae**

The Celestial is native to South Texas and confined to this region. It is also the only species of this genus in Texas. It grows 10-30 cm high with narrow pleated leaves 8-25 cm long. The "flower" comprises tepals—not petals, but beautiful tepals they are. It is frequent on sand or clay in prairies and grasslands, blooming from March to May.

# WATER HYACINTH

*Eichhornia crassipes*

**Water-Hyacinth Family: Pontederiaceae**

This water-growing plant floats on the surface of rivers, lakes, and other waterways, frequently forming large masses. In many places it is a serious pest, introduced from South America. Water-hyacinth blooms from May to November with a beauty that even the illustration cannot replicate. Another species, *E. azurea,* may also be found in South Texas; but it is not, for the purposes of this guide, significantly different.

# PASSIONFLOWER

*Passiflora foetida*

**Passionflower Family: Passifloraceae**

An ill-scented, annual, ground-covering vine with stems to 6 m in length and three-lobed leaves 4-7 cm wide and as long. The feathery petals are about 1.5 cm long and may also be white. The fruits, not edible, are 2-2.5 cm wide, turning red when ripe. Flowering from April to November, it is frequent in thickets, pastures, woods, and waste places where water is plentiful. Other passionflowers are found in this area; one, Maypop or *P. incarnata,* has edible fruits.

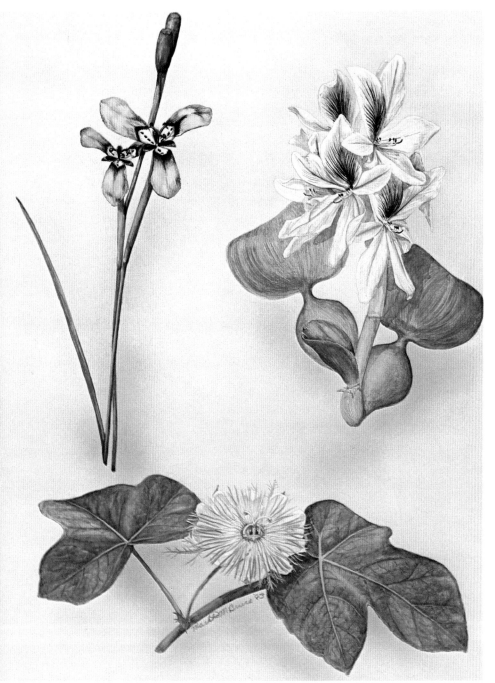

PASSIONFLOWER

# BLUE-EYED GRASS

*Sisyrinchium pruinosum*

**Iris Family: Iridaceae**

A genus with many species and some affinity for hybridization makes a floral key for definite identification a requirement. *S. pruinosum* is, however, common in South Texas, occurring on sands and clays and tending to form clumps. This species is a perennial with erect stems of 8-30 cm and blooming from March to May. Tepals, not petals, provide the color. *S. minus* is another common find; its tepals are purple-rose.

# SPIDERWORT

*Tradescantia occidentalis*

**Spiderwort Family: Commelinaceae**

*Occidentalis* is one of a number of species in this genus; all are perennials and some require a floral key to identify species. Some perhaps produce interspecific hybrids. This species grows to 80 cm high with leaves to 40 cm or more in length. It can be very abundant in the area where it is growing and will be found on various soils in prairies, openings, and waste places as well as along roads. It may begin blooming in February and continues until June or later with petals of 1.5-2 cm long.

# SANDBELL

*Nama hispidum*

**Waterleaf Family: Hydrophyllaceae**

This widespread species, not restricted to South Texas, is highly variable in form. It is an annual with much-branched stems that are erect or spreading and may reach 30 cm in height. The corolla is 8-12 mm long and may be pink or bright purple. Sandbell is frequent on sandy and gravelly soils, blooming from March to July.

BLUE-EYED GRASS                    SPIDERWORT

SANDBELL

# MEALYCUP SAGE

*Salvia farinacea*

**Mint Family: Lamiaceae (Labiatae)**

Also known as Mealy Sage, this species is a perennial to 1 m high with leaves 3-9 cm long. The corolla is about 1.5 cm long. There is, or was, an extensive dense stand of this sage just south of Goliad, Texas. In general it is found on caliche soils in our area. It blooms from March to November.

# BLUE CURLS

*Phacelia congesta*

**Waterleaf Family: Hydrophyllaceae**

Another of the Blue Curls, this one occurs not only in our area but also throughout the state, except East Texas, and into other southwestern states and Mexico. It grows to about 1 m tall and has leaves 2-12 cm long with two or three leaflets or more per leaf. The flowers are generally colored as depicted; one variety has white flowers, with a corolla 7-9 mm wide. A frequently seen species, it blooms from March to April.

# BLUE SAGE

*Salvia texana*

**Mint Family: Lamiaceae (Labiatae)**

A perennial to 30 to 40 cm high, with several stems that are themselves branched, this sage has leaves 3-9 cm long. The corolla is about 1.5 cm long. It has a wide distribution in the state and northern Mexico on caliche or limestone soils. This places it in the western portion of our area, where it blooms from March to November.

MEALYCUP SAGE

BLUE CURLS

BLUE SAGE

# BLUEBONNET

*Lupinus subcarnosus*

**Pea Family: Fabaceae (Leguminosae)**

This native species and the similar *L. texensis* and other varieties of bluebonnet are recognized as the state flower of Texas. Both species occur in abundance, particularly along roadsides where they have been planted by the highway department and other groups. Both *subcarnosus* and *texensis* are annuals, branching from the base, 15-40 cm tall with leaves of 4-7 leaflets. In both the upper petal is 8-12 mm long, and both bloom from February to April. *Subcarnosus* is more likely to be found on sandy soils.

# BLUE STAR

*Gilia rigidula*

**Phlox Family: Polemoniaceae**

This perennial occurs on the western half of our area on dry sands or caliche. There are several subspecies and one other very similiar species, *G. ludens;* only the subspecies *rigidula* and the species *ludens* are to be encountered in our area. In general *rigidula* will have spreading branches to 25 cm tall and a corolla 1.5-2 cm wide that is blue or violet-blue. It is a most attractive flower blooming chiefly from March to May, occasionally in the fall. *G. incisa* may also be found. It grows to 60 cm in height and has a pale blue-violet corolla less than 1 cm wide.

# WIDOW'S TEARS

*Commelina erecta*

**Spiderwort Family: Commelinaceae**

This perennial herb's stems trail or sprawl to 60 or more cm long. Several species occur in our area. If the smaller petal below the two big blue ones is white, the plant is *C. erecta;* if the smaller petal is blue, the flower is *C. diffusa.* Widow's Tears are common on various soils, at times forming dense growths. Hierba del Pollo, as it is also known, blooms from March through December.

WIDOW'S TEARS

# PRAIRIE NYMPH

*Alophia drummondii (Eustylis purpurea)*

**Iris Family: Iridaceae**

A beautiful Iris, the Prairie Nymph is a perennial 20-60 cm high or more with narrow pleated leaves 5-40 cm long. It is frequent on sandy soils in prairies and in openings. The colorful "flower" is formed by tepals, not petals. Called by some Purple Pleat-Leaf, this sole Texas representative of the genus blooms from April to October.

# SILVERLEAF NIGHTSHADE

*Solanum elaeagnifolium*

**Nightshade Family: Solanaceae**

One of a number of species in this genus, *S. elaeagniolium* is easily recognizable and common. It is perennial with thorny or prickly stems, found in colonies. Occasionally reaching 1 m in height, it is often assigned the status of weed. The silver or gray coloration of the leaves and stems comes from a covering of many short hairs. The corolla is 2-4 cm wide and occasionally white. It is also commonly called Trompillo and may be found in bloom from April to November.

# PIMPERNEL

*Anagallis arvensis*

**Primrose Family: Primulaceae**

This flower is a native of Europe but is frequently found along roadsides and in prairies, fields, and waste places. Petal color can vary from scarlet to salmon or blue to almost white. The flowers occur individually on pedicels and are variable in size but generally about 1 cm wide. This annual plant will flower while very small but also forms loose prostrate mats. Other common names are Scarlet Pimpernel and Hierba Del Pajaro. The only species of this genus in Texas, it flowers from March to May or June.

PRAIRIE NYMPH

SILVERLEAF NIGHTSHADE

PIMPERNEL

39

# GLOBE MALLOW

*Sphaeralcea pedatifida*

**Mallow Family: Malvaceae**

This is a biennial, living two years, or weak perennial 30-70 cm high with upright or reclining stems. The leaves are 1.5-4 cm long and lobed. There are 12 species of *Sphaeralcea* but most occur in West Texas. *S. pedatifida* is one of three or four to be found in our area. It is frequent on sand in prairies and openings, and also to be found on rocky or gravelly slopes. The petals are 8-12 mm long. It blooms chiefly from March to May; some may continue until October.

# FLAX

*Linum rigidum*

**Flax Family: Linaceae**

There are many species of Flax in Texas and several in South Texas. *L. rigidum* is a perennial with upright or reclining stems up to 35 cm long. The petals are 1.5-2 cm long and usually reddish toward the base. This species is frequent on various soils and blooms from February to June. All of the flaxes found in our area will have yellow or orange-yellow as the major color of the petals except for *L. usitatissimum,* which is the cultivated variety with blue flowers. It occasionally escapes and is found growing wild.

# GLOBE MALLOW

*Sphaeralcea lindheimeri*

**Mallow Family: Malvaceae**

Another mallow in South Texas, *S. lindheimeri* is a perennial with ascending or reclining stems as long as 75 cm. The leaves are 1.5-6 cm long and frequently lobed as shown. The petals are 1.5-2 cm long. It is frequent on deep sand both inland and along the coast. This species is endemic, restricted to South Texas. Beginning to bloom as early as February and continuing until December in some cases, it is common from March to May.

GLOBE MALLOW

# BROWN-EYED SUSAN

*Rudbeckia hirta*

**Sunflower Family: Asteraceae (Compositae)**

A genus with seven Texas species, only *R. hirta* is likely to be encountered in South Texas. Two varieties of the species grow here. Both are annuals or weak perennials to 60 cm high with leaves 2-10 cm long and solitary flower heads 3-5 cm wide. Var. *angustifolia* generally branches at or near the middle of the plant and is frequent in deep sands of coastal oak woods and on the barrier islands. Var. *pulcherrima* generally branches above the middle of the plant and is occasionally locally abundant in prairies, openings, and waste places on sands and sandy clays. They both bloom from April to July. Another species, *Dracopis amplexicaulis* has a flower very similar to *R. hirta* and is also called Brown-eyed Susan.

# MEXICAN HAT

*Ratibida columnaris*

**Sunflower Family: Asteraceae (Compositae)**

This common perennial, 20-75 cm high, has solitary flowering heads 3-5 cm wide. The petal-like ray flowers can vary from red-brown tipped with yellow to solid red-brown or solid yellow. The cone portion is usually dark brown. It is a very noticeable wildflower occurring over a wide area on clay or clayey soils and caliche. It blooms chiefly from April to June although it may also be found in the fall.

# INDIAN BLANKET

*Gaillardia pulchella*

**Sunflower Family: Asteraceae (Compositae)**

This annual herb grows up to 60 cm tall, usually with branches from near the base. The flowering heads are 3.5-5.5 cm wide and display a wide variety of petal coloration. The ray flowers, those surrounding the central disk, vary from solid red to red tipped with yellow to solid yellow. It is one of the most common and characteristic of the spring flowers and can cover fields and roadsides. *Pulchella* prefers sunshine and is most frequent in the spring and early summer on sandy soils and prairies. It is also called Firewheel.

BROWN-EYED SUSAN                                    MEXICAN HAT

INDIAN BLANKET

# SOW THISTLE

*Sonchus oleraceus*

**Sunflower Family: Asteraceae (Compositae)**

There are two species of Sow Thistle in Texas. Both are visually much alike. *S. asper* and the pictured *S. oleraceus* are annuals growing up to 1.2 m tall, though they are frequently seen flowering much shorter. The flowering heads are 1.5-2.8 cm wide. To identify the species, the akenes, or "seeds" must be examined. If the akene is smooth the plant is *oleraceus;* if cross-wrinkled, it is *asper*. Both plants are frequent on various soils, often being weedy pests. Natives of Europe, they are chiefly cool-season plants, growing and blooming mostly from October to May.

# MEXICAN POPPY

*Argemone mexicana*

**Poppy Family: Papaveraceae**

A prickly, stinging, erect herbaceous annual to 60 cm or more high, with leaves 2.5-8 cm long. The petals are 2-3 cm long. Very similar in appearance to *A. sanguinea* but less common, it is an occasional find along roads and in waste places. It is a native of the West Indies that blooms from March to June. Several other common names are used for this plant: Devil's Fig, Yellow Prickly Poppy, Cardo Santo, and Chicalote.

# FALSE DANDELION

*Pyrrhopappus multicaulis*

**Sunflower Family: Asteraceae (Compositae)**

This annual, 15-65 cm high, displays much variability and apparently hybridizes with *P. carolinianus*. It is common on various soils and blooms from February to June. Three species in this genus may be encountered, and a floral key is necessary to segregate them.

SOW THISTLE                                    MEXICAN POPPY

FALSE DANDELION

# HUISACHE DAISY

*Amblyolepis setigera*

**Sunflower Family: Asteraceae (Compositae)**

This annual grows 30 cm high with leaves 2-6 cm long and solitary heads 3-4 cm wide. It is frequent on sandy soils or caliche in prairies and openings. An attractive flower, it blooms from February to June.

# SQUARE-BUD DAISY

*Tetragonotheca repanda*

**Sunflower Family: Asteraceae (Compositae)**

A perennial to 60 cm tall, it is one of two species in this genus found in South Texas. The leaves are 7-12 cm long and the flowering heads are solitary, 1.5-2 cm wide. As the name implies, the flower buds are noticeably angular. It is frequent on deep sand and sandy prairies where it is endemic to South Texas. It flowers from March to November. *T. texana* is the other species that may be encountered. It is of similar appearance but prefers to grow on ridges in calcareous soils.

# WILD INDIGO

*Baptisia leucophaea*

**Pea Family: Fabaceae (Leguminosae)**

One of four species in the genus to be found in Texas, this perennial is the only one likely to be found in South Texas. It grows to 50 cm or more high with three 4-8-cm-long leaflets per leaf. A frequent find on deep sands in prairies and openings or on the barrier islands, it may bloom as early as January but most often is found from March to May. The plant in South Texas will be variety *laevicaulis*.

HUISACHE DAISY                    SQUARE-BUD DAISY

WILD INDIGO

47

# EVENING-PRIMROSE

*Calylophus berlandieri (Calylophus drummondianus)*

**Evening-Primrose Family: Onagraceae**

In this confusing genus of five species, *C. berlandieri* is one of three found in South Texas. A bushy to erect perennial to annual 10-50 cm tall with leaves 1-8 cm long, it is broken into two subspecies. Ours is *C. b. berlandieri*. The petals are 14-22 mm long. It occurs frequently on sandy soils or sometimes caliche in prairies and openings and blooms from March to November. Because so many Evening-primroses abound, consult a floral key for a definite identification of a flower that doesn't look like the one pictured. The Evening-primroses may be quickly separated into genera by examining the stigma. The stigma of *Calylophus* will be disk-shaped and that of *Oenothera* split into five individual parts.

# TICKSEED

*Coreopsis nuecensis*

**Sunflower Family: Asteraceae (Compositae)**

An annual 20-60 cm tall, the leaves are variable but frequently are segmented into three to five "leaflets." The heads are solitary, 3-5 cm wide. A species of the genus called Tickseed, *C. nuecensis* is frequent and sometimes abundant on sands and sandy loams. The reddish markings on the petals make this an easy plant to identify. It blooms from February to May.

# EVENING-PRIMROSE

*Calylophus hartwegii*

**Evening-Primrose Family: Onagraceae**

This perennial has reclining or upright stems and leaves 1-4 cm long. Of the six subspecies described, *C. h. maccartii* is the one found in South Texas. The flowers are yellow and the petals are 1.5-2 cm long. It is frequent on dry sand or caliche in the more western portions of the area. It blooms from March to October.

EVENING-PRIMROSE

# WATER PRIMROSE

*Ludwigia peploides*

**Evening-Primrose Family: Onagraceae**

A genus of 12 species in Texas, all associated with water or damp places, *L. peploides* is a perennial with creeping, trailing, or floating stems 1.8 m or more long. The leaves are 2-8 cm long. The petals are 1.2-2 cm long and the plant blooms from April to November. Its Spanish name is Verdolaga de Agua.

# PUCCOON

*Lithospermum incisum*

**Heliotrope Family: Boraginaceae**

One of three or four species of the genus found in Texas, *L. incisum* is a perennial to 20 cm or more in height, with leaves from 2 to 12 cm long. It is an upright plant with flowers borne in clusters, the corolla 9-20 mm wide and ruffled. It is frequent on sandy or clayey loams in prairies and openings and blooms from March to April.

# BLADDERPOD

*Lesquerella lasiocarpa*

**Mustard Family: Brassicaceae (Cruciferae)**

One of a large number of species in this genus, *L. lasiocarpa* is an annual with reclining or prostrate stems to 60 cm long, leaves 1-10 cm long. The petals of the flowers are 6-10 mm long. It is frequent on sandy and clayey soils over a large area and blooms from January to May. Four or more species may be encountered; a floral key is necessary to separate them.

BLADDERPOD

# GREEN-THREAD

*Thelesperma ambiguum*

**Sunflower Family: Asteraceae (Compositae)**

Similar to *Coreopsis tinctoria, T. ambiguum* is a perennial growing 40 cm high with leaves divided into segments. The heads are solitary, 2.5-5 cm wide. This genus can be separated from *Coreopsis* by the width of the leaf segments. If the segments are mostly less than 2 mm wide and the choice is between *Thelesperma* and *Coreopsis,* it is *Thelesperma.* Flowering March through November, it is frequent on caliche or dry sand. Two other *Thelesperma, T. filifolium* and *T. nuecense* are generally similar. They occur more along the coast on sand or shell around beaches.


# GOLDEN WAVE

*Coreopsis tinctoria*

**Sunflower Family: Asteraceae (Compositae)**

As pictured, this species is similar in appearance to *Thelesperma ambiguum.* It is an annual to 50 cm high with segmented leaves. The heads are 2-3 cm wide and solitary. The leaf segments are 2 mm wide or more. It is found in low, damp areas such as ditches by the side of the road and is occasionally seen in large patches. It blooms almost year round but most heavily in the spring. *C. basalis,* another frequent *Coreopsis* found in our area, is not quite as tall, has a generally larger (3.5-5 cm) head, and is found on deep sands.


# COMMON SUNFLOWER

*Helianthus annuus*

**Sunflower Family: Asteraceae (Compositae)**

The Common Sunflower is one of 16 or so species in this genus occurring in Texas. The variety pictured is *texanus.* It grows to 2 m or more tall with leaves 6-30 cm long. It is common on clay or heavier sands in a wide area. Also called Mirasol, it blooms from March to December.


*This illustration displays three DYC's or "Darn" Yellow Comps., (another category is DWC's, "Darn" White Comps.), often the bane of the budding or even journeyman taxonomist. The family Asteracae (formerly Compositae), Sunflower or Daisy, is one of the largest in the plant kingdom and it is often difficult to separate all those daisies.*

GREEN-THREAD                                                  GOLDEN WAVE

SUNFLOWER

# OLD PLAINSMAN

*Hymenopappus scabiosaeus*

**Sunflower Family: Asteraceae (Compositae)**

There are a number of species in this genus, which is known as Wooly-White. Pictured is the variety *corymbosus*, which is widespread in and beyond South Texas on clay soils. As it grows to 60 cm or more in height and is often rather isolated, it is quite conspicuous. The flowering heads are 7-13 mm high. This biennial blooms from March to June or July.

# PRICKLY POPPY

*Argemone sanguinea*

**Poppy Family: Papaveraceae**

A prickly, stinging, erect herbaceous annual to 1 m or more high, this species has two color phases, white and purple or lavender, with petals 3-4 cm long. In some areas it is an abundant although attractive pest. It occurs in disturbed areas and fields on various soils and frequently along roadsides. It may also be called Red Poppy.

# LAZY DAISY

*Aphanostephus skirrhobasis*

**Sunflower Family: Asteraceae (Compositae)**

An annual DWC (see explanation on page 50), *A. skirrhobasis* grows from 5 to 45 cm high with leaves 1-6 cm long. The heads are usually 2-3.5 cm wide, blooming from February to November. The variety pictured is *thallasius*, which has a low-spreading habit. It is common on sandy soils in prairies, openings, and waste places, including roadsides. Several other species in this genus may be encountered.

LAZY DAISY

# PINK DANDELION

*Pinaropappus roseus*

**Sunflower Family: Asteraceae (Compositae)**

While known as the Pink Dandelion, *P. roseus* often occurs with white petals as pictured here. It may also have pink or lavender petals and even the white color phase is often tinged with pink. It is a perennial 10-30 cm tall, occasionally 45 cm, with leaves 4-15 cm long crowded around the base of the stem. It is not infrequent on clay, sandy loam, or caliche, sometimes lightly shaded. The showy flowering head, 3-5 cm wide, is borne singly on the stalk. Blooming from March to May, it is known in other areas as Rock-lettuce.

# SMARTWEED

*Polygonum hydropiperoides (Persicaria hydropiperoides)*

**Buckwheat Family: Polygonaceae**

There are many species of Smartweed in Texas, six or more occurring in South Texas. *P. hydropiperoides* is a perennial or annual with erect stems to 1 m high. The leaves are 4-12 cm long. The flowers are 1.5-3 mm long and may also be pinkish. Several other species closely resemble one another, and a floral key is necessary to make definite identifications. The Smartweeds in general grow in shallow water or along the edges of bodies of water. *P. hydropiperoides* is a frequent find, blooming from April to December.

# TEXAS FROG FRUIT

*Phyla incisa*

**Verbena Family: Verbenaceae**

An easily recognized genus with several similar species in South Texas, *P. incisa* is a prostrate mat-forming perennial whose stems grow to 60 cm long. The leaves are 1-4 cm long. The flowers are in compact heads, white to pale lavender, with the corolla 2-3.5 mm wide. It is frequent on various soils in prairies, openings, waste places, and along roads. It blooms from April to November.

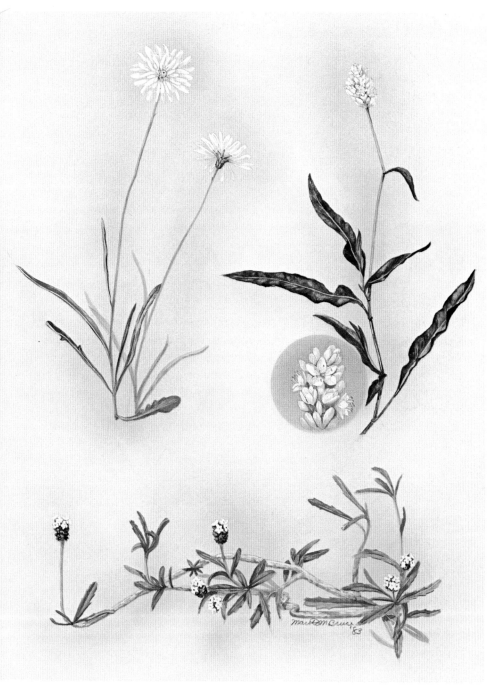

TEXAS FROG FRUIT

# PRAIRIE LARKSPUR

*Delphinium virescens*

**Buttercup Family: Ranunculaceae**

Of the six described species of *Delphinium* in Texas, two native and one introduced species may be found in South Texas. *D. virescens*, pictured, is a native perennial to 75 cm high. Its leaves are usually divided into three lobes, themselves divided again. A frequent find on sandy and clayey soils or caliche, it blooms from March to May. The flowers, including the spur on the back end, are up to 4 cm long and may be light blue-lavender as well as white. The plant is also called White or Plains Larkspur. *D. carolinianum* is less frequently encountered. Its flowers are deep violet-blue and 2-3 cm long. *D. ajacis* L. is a cultivated species, native to Europe, which has escaped and can be found along roadsides and in waste places. The flowers range from bright blue to violet, purple, pink, or white.

# WILD ONION

*Allium canadense*

**Lily Family: Lilaceae**

There are several species of *Allium* in Texas, perhaps four in our area. The species pictured also has several varieties described. Shown is variety *mobilense*. Its flowering stalk is 35 cm or more high with 25 to 75 flowers. As with the other *Allium* the "flower" is formed by tepals 4-7 mm long, not petals. Not common but unusually attractive, it occurs on deep sands and blooms from April to May. As noted, there are several species and varieties of *Allium* around; and a floral key is recommended for positive identification.

# ALAMO VINE

*Ipomoea sinuata*

**Morning-Glory Family: Convolvulaceae**

Of the 33 described species of *Ipomoea* in Texas, many occur in South Texas. However, if the flowers are white with a purple throat and the leaves are thin and divided as shown, the species is probably *I. sinuata*. Like most Morning-glories in South Texas, this one is a vine with stems to 3 m or more long. The corolla is 3-4.5 cm long. A perennial found in many places, this plant is also cultivated. It blooms from April until November. Morning-glories as a group are easy to recognize; for identification at the species level a floral key is required. This species, in the future, may be designated *Merremia dissecta*.

ALAMO VINE

# DEWBERRY

*Rubus trivialis*

**Rose Family: Rosaceae**

Of the many species in this genus, *R. trivialis* will be most commonly encountered in South Texas. It is an extremely prickly/thorny, woody-based evergreen shrub forming a dense tangled thicket up to 2 m high. There are 3-5 leaflets per leaf. The flower petals are 10-15 mm long. The fruits are formed in a globular cluster and are quite good to eat when ripe. A native of China also called Southern Dewberry or Zarzamora, it blooms generally from May to June in our area.


# CONVOLVULUS

*Convolvulus equitans*

**Morning-glory Family: Convolvulaceae**

This perennial vine has trailing, twining stems up to 2 m or more long and leaves mostly 2-6 cm long. The flowers are solitary; the corolla is 1-3.5 cm long and lavender as well as white. Both colors may display a red throat. This frequent find on loamy soils or caliche in openings, prairies, and waste places, blooms from March to November. *C. arvensis* is a similar plant. It is a native of Eurasia and forms large patches, occasionally several acres in extent, choking out other plants. It blooms from April through November.


# BLUET

*Hedyotis nigricans*

**Madder Family: Rubiaceae**

This perennial has erect to spreading stems up to 40 cm long and leaves 1-4 cm long. The corolla is 5-9 mm wide, white to lavender or light violet. Blooming from April to November, it is frequent on dry, calcareous soils and on beach shell. It is also a species that displays a great deal of variability. Many species belong to this genus, all commonly called Bluets, many occurring in South Texas. A floral key is suggested to make positive identifications.

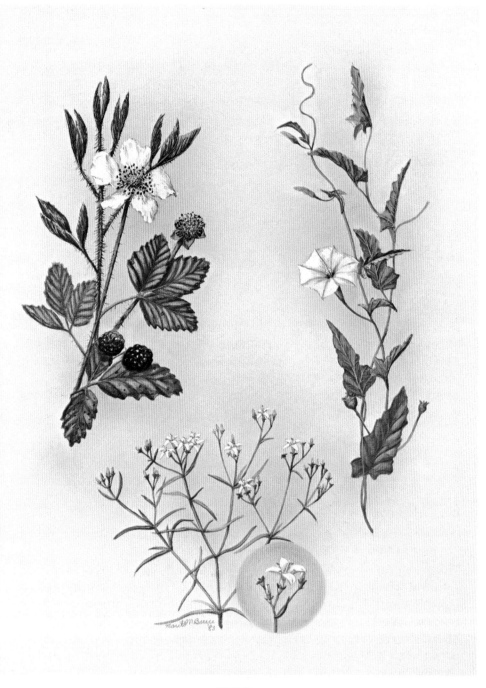

BLUET

# QUEEN ANN'S LACE

*Ammi majus*

**Carrot Family: Apiaceae (Umbelliferae)**

This frequently cultivated introduction from Eurasia has escaped to road-sides and waste places. It is a tall, to 1.7 m, erect annual plant with leaves 6-20 cm long divided into leaflets. The petals are 1-2 mm long. A very noticeable plant, it blooms in April and May.

# SPIDER LILY

*Hymenocallis liriosme*

**Amaryllis Family: Amaryllidaceae**

Found in low areas and around rivers, streams, ponds, and in general wet places, this species is usually 40-60 cm high with 4 to 11 flowers on each stem. The tepals are the colorful showy portion of the "flower." The tepals are 8-12 cm long. A fairly frequent find, it will occasionally form dense growths of extensive area, as in old pond bottoms. It blooms from March to May. Two other species in this genus occur in Texas and might be encountered in the northern and eastern portions of South Texas: *H. euale,* which blooms from July to September, and *H. caroliniana,* which blooms from March to May. The leaves of *H. caroliniana* are generally 18-42 cm wide; those of *H. liriosme* commonly less than 20 cm wide.

# BULL NETTLE

*Cnidoscolus texanus*

**Spurge Family: Euphorbiaceae**

Growing nearly throughout this state and in several other states and Mexico, this perennial herb is the only one in its genus to be found in Texas. The plant grows to 80 cm high; both leaves and stems are thickly provided with stinging bristles, whose effect lingers long after the plant has been released. It occurs frequently enough to be a pest in many areas. Growing chiefly on deep sands in prairies and openings, it also appears on the barrier islands. It begins blooming around March and continues until November.

QUEEN ANN'S LACE                    SPIDER LILY

BULL NETTLE

# LADIES TRESSES

*Spiranthes vernalis*

**Orchid Family: Orchidaceae**

This perennial, growing to 40 cm or more high, has fleshy narrow leaves. The perianth, petals and sepals as a unit, is 5-8 mm long. Found frequently in low moist grounds chiefly along the coast and on the barrier islands, *S. vernalis* blooms from April to June. It is of several species of *Spiranthes* that might be encountered in South Texas.

# MILKWORT

*Polygala alba*

**Milkwort Family: Polygalaceae**

One of many species in this genus, collectively known as Milkworts, *P. alba* is a perennial with upright or spreading stems 50 cm long and narrow leaves 8-15 mm long. The flowers are 3-4 mm long and are sometimes purplish. One other South Texas species, *P. verticillata* has flowers that are normally white, and smaller, about 1.5 mm long; and the plant is only about 20 cm high. *P. alba* is a multistemmed plant that grows on dry sand or caliche or on the barrier islands and occasionally on clay. It is frequently seen blooming from March to November.

# ARROWHEAD

*Sagittaria longiloba*

**Waterplantain Family: Alismataceae**

The genus as a whole is called Arrowheads; this species is known as Flecha de Agua. As in most of the rest of the genus *S. longiloba* is a perennial rooted in the bottom. The leaves display a great variety of shapes and the flowers are borne in whorls of three, the petals 8-16 mm long. There are several species found in South Texas, all with white flowers. The genus, which has edible roots, was a staple food of Indians and also used by settlers. *S. longiloba* blooms from April to December.

ARROWHEAD

# WILDFLOWERS: FACTS & FOLKTALES

Dr. E. R. Bogusch, Professor Emeritus of biology at Texas A&I University, with the assistance of his wife Ethel Bogusch, has contributed the following folklore and interesting facts on a few of the flowers described previously.

### Firewheel                                                                    *Gaillardia*

The Firewheel or Indian Blanket, *Gaillardia pulchella,* occupies the traditional hunting grounds of the Comanche Indians. A delightful legend, said to come from the Comanches, concerns the adventures of an Indian youth and the daughter of a chief who became separated from a hunting party one warm March afternoon. According to the legend, the warm and mellow afternoon sun became covered with sullen clouds, dark and brooding, and the icy fingers of the wind sent chills through the youngsters' bodies.

Soon, the lost children realized they would perish unless aid came quickly. They looked frantically for some sort of shelter. Finally they crawled under the dense green carpet of Firewheel. Slowly the storm abated during the tumultuous night until at sunrise the new golden light matched that of the Firewheel's brilliance.

When the Indian Chief saw his children safe, he called for the blessing of the Great Spirit and asked that all the flowers which had sheltered the children be given a part of the sun's golden light as a sign. Even today it is said that one can tell which were the plants blessed by the Great Spirit because each carries an omen from the sun — a yellow tip of the showy flowers.

### Nightshade                                                                    *Solanum*

*Solanum* is represented by a large number of related species in Texas. Some grow to resemble the potato and bear the name of wild potato. These wild species are toxic and can cause severe gastric disturbances. Certain species of *Solanum* may produce red or light-colored berries; others are blue or purple. When originally discovered by botanists the tomato was considered poisonous because it is a *Solanum.* People a hundred years ago grew it as an ornamental plant and called it the love apple. Even though the wild tomato plant looks much like a nightshade, it is the ancestor of our much-liked table tomato.

## Anemone

The several species of Anemone found to grow naturally in South Texas are now considered to be closely related to the Asiatic species that grow as spring flowers in the Holy Land. Indeed, botanists have identified practically all plants mentioned in the Bible. They are of the opinion that the "lilies of the field" are Old World forms of an ancient group of flowering plants.

## Bluebonnet                                                           *Lupinus*

Both common species of the Texas Bluebonnet show a tally of visits from nectar-seeking bees. On the pealike flower of the bluebonnet there is one petal, the standard, much larger than the rest. An observer watching a bee can readily note that there are flowers near the middle of the floral spike where the bee pauses only a moment, and then goes on. In almost every case these flowers have a red spot near the center of the standard. These flowers are already pollinated. The bee seems to know that they have no nectar. The bee will visit the flowers that have a white spot on the standard. As she harvests the nectar she pollinates the blossom. Thus, a calling card hurries up the bee's business.

## Stork's Bill                                                          *Erodium*

The wild geranium, *Erodium texanum,* is not to be confused with its cultivated relative, which bears the name of geranium as well. The wild species can be readily distinguished by its pointed beaklike mature fruit, which gives it the name of Stork's Bill. Each segment of the maturing fruit separates into parts that fall to the ground and twist into a tight spiral. The seed that is attached to the twisting part is screwed into the ground, as it were, to become effectively planted. This plant takes no chances.

# GLOSSARY

**Akene** (achene)  A hard one-seeded fruit. In this book pertaining to flowers in the Asteraceae (Sunflower) Family. A sunflower seed, unshelled, is an akene.

**Annual**  A plant that grows, flowers, and dies in one year.

**Biennial**  A plant that grows for two years, generally flowering in the second, and then dies

**Corolla**  The petals of a flower.

**Caliche**  A whitish rock-like concretion of calcium carbonates or magnesium carbonates formed under certain soils. It may form a hardpan or be more dispersed. It is often exposed by erosion. It is used in many places as a road-making material.

**Endemic**  Found only in a restricted geographic area.

**Pedicel**  The stalk of an individual flower in a cluster of flowers.

**Peduncle**  The stalk of a flower cluster or a single flower if it represents a reduced flower cluster.

**Perennial**  A plant that grows at least more than two years, normally for several to many years.

**Pistle**  The female portion of the flower, consisting of the ovary and the stigma with generally a style between the two.

**Prostrate**  Being flat on the ground.

**Raceme**  An arrangement of flowers along a single major peduncle, with each flower having a pedicel.

**Rhizome**  An undergound stem; that is, **not** a root. It has nodes and often produces roots and shoots.

**Rosette**  A cluster of leaves surrounding the base of the plant.

**Sepal**  A generally leaf-like part of the flower just below the corolla.

**Spike**  A group of flowers on a peduncle, each flower not having a pedicel — that is, not stemmed.

**Stigma**  The female portion of the flower, the top portion of the pistle, to which pollen adheres.

**Style**  A generally stalk-like part connecting the stigma and ovary.

**Swale**  A low area where water collects and remains for some time after a rain.

**Tepal**  A flower part that combines the appearance of a sepal and a petal.

# INDEX

# INDEX

*Prior names which have been revised.

The darkened area of the map indicates the major area of South Texas covered by this book. Most of the flowers are fairly widespread through South Texas.